# HANDBOOK ON FAITH, HOPE, AND LOVE

## Saint Augustine

*Translated by Albert C. Outler*

**RELEVANT BOOKS**

Published by RELEVANT Books
A division of RELEVANT Media Group, Inc.

www.relevantbooks.com
www.relevantmediagroup.com

© 2006 RELEVANT Media Group

Design by RELEVANT Solutions
Cover design by Ben Pieratt
Cover illustration by Anna Melcon
Interior design by Ben Pieratt, Jeremy Kennedy, Anna Melcon, Aaron Maurer

For information or bulk orders:
RELEVANT MEDIA GROUP, INC.
100 SOUTH LAKE DESTINY DR., STE 200
ORLANDO, FL 32810
407-660-1411

Library of Congress Control Number: 2005911199
International Standard Book Number: 0-9776167-0-3

06 07 08 09 10 8 7 6 5 4 3 2 1

Printed in the United States of America

This book is a brief handbook or *enchiridion* on the proper mode of serving God, through *Faith, Hope,* and *Love.*

# CONTENTS

# INTRODUCTION

Recently, I was in conversation with a friend who was wrestling over those perpetual questions of knowing God's mind and making wise choices amid life-altering options, the same sorts of questions that have kept most of us in a fog at some point or another. My concluding advice was to quote Saint Augustine: "Love God, and do as you please." With raised eyebrows, he sat back and said, "Bold words." His tone and body language suggested he might have just heard something scandalous. I told him Augustine was a Church father born in the fourth century who had earned the right to be trusted, even though his words were indeed bold and dangerous.

Trust is a depleting commodity these days. Information is cheap, and little of it has any staying power; little of it has any more value than the bandwidth providing its digital home. We hear so much that, over time, it all begins to sound the same. It's just loud, annoying noise, and we trust little of it to be deeply true or inherently meaningful. There is a unique voice, however, that comes only with age, with words that have echoed through the centuries. This well-aged voice crackles with authenticity, and there is something about it that is so alive, so wise and tested—so current, even—that the matter of trust is simply not a question. Saint Augustine of Hippo has such a voice.

In 354, Augustine was born in the city of Tagaste, in a North African province of the Roman Empire. He was trained in rhetoric and philosophy and had a brilliant mind, securing academic elitism by the age of thirty. But Augustine was no dull prude. He knew wealth and experienced prominence and power. His sexual prowess has been much discussed, and it was during the years of his promiscuity that he offered his sardonic prayer, "Grant me chastity and continence, but not yet." In 386, however, Augustine went through a dramatic conversion, abandoning his academic career, committing to celibacy and the priesthood, and surrendering himself to a life of serving Christ and the Church. He left behind a number of published works, the most well-known of which are the autobiographical *Confessions* and *The City of God*, his tome dealing with Christianity's relation to and distinction from the broader Roman culture.

Augustine's *Handbook on Faith, Hope, and Love* is a smaller volume written in response to a letter from a man we know only as Laurence, one of his devotees who had written to Augustine asking for spiritual guidance. Laurence had rattled off a series of questions: How can one properly serve God? How can one know the core of how to please God? What role does reason play in faith? What can we be absolutely certain of? All good questions. Remarkably, all modern questions. In true philosophical fashion, Augustine turned the questions around and suggested the answers to each could be found by answering three other questions: What should we believe? What should we hope for? What should we love? These are the essentials we must attend to, Augustine would tell Laurence—faith, hope, and love.

Augustine was a philosopher from another age, and at times, his thought can be difficult to follow. One should not, however, mistake his density for sterility. At the outset of his response, Augustine warned Laurence that "if one is to have wisdom, it is not enough just to put an enchiridion [Augustine's word for the sort of book he was writing] in the hand. It is also necessary that a great zeal be kindled in the heart." This remark provides us with one of the essential elements of any voice that is still able to offer us timely clarity 1,700 years after it was first heard. An enduring voice inevitably possesses the quality of stirring our heart as profoundly as it stirs our mind.

Augustine would be most pleased, I imagine, if his ancient words give us more than historical insight into a bygone era or a cerebral conversation with an old sage. Augustine's central passion was God and His supreme goodness. I am certain Augustine would take great delight if we encounter in his musings on faith, hope, and love "glimpses of that ineffable beauty whose full vision is our highest happiness." It is some of these rawer places, discussions around beauty and desire, where I find Augustine most compelling. He speaks of how the human soul, despite its broken and fallen state, can never "lose its appetite for blessedness," and he is forever reminding us that it is only in God where this blessedness—this intense thirst for pleasure—is realized.

Augustine's wisdom does not emerge from his infallibility. He would never claim as much, and certainly the long years since his death have provided ample opportunities to critique many of his views. "Every man ought to speak what is in his heart—not only when he himself knows the truth, but even when he errs and is deceived, as a man may be," said Augustine. It is this honesty, this commitment to offering one's heart selflessly, that offers an instructive model for our own journey into God. Are we on the path? Do we move? Do we risk? Do we give what we have come to believe, even when we are fully aware that our frailty and imperfection muddle our clarity? Part of Augustine's long-standing appeal is this integrity, grappling with the reality of what it means to be human while consistently reordering us toward what is even more true, more fundamentally alive, than our most basic humanness. Augustine is continually busy reordering our mind and our affections toward God.

In Augustine, then, we find a sturdy guide, one who clearly knows who and where we are: humans in desperate need of God. May his words give us a voice for some of our own longings, and may his delight in God kindle in us a desire for delights of our own.

Winn Collier
Author of *Restless Faith*

# BIOGRAPHY OF SAINT AUGUSTINE

**Full Name:** Aurelius Augustinus, Saint Augustine of Hippo

**Date of Birth:** November 13, 354 CE

**Family Stats:** His mother, Saint Monica, was a devout Christian. His father, Patricius, was a pagan. He had one son, born to his concubine.

**Lived In:** Carthage as a child, studied in Rome, taught in Milan, spent the end of his life as bishop of Hippo

**Occupation:** Professor of rhetoric, bishop of Hippo

**Claim to Fame:** His book *Confessions* is often considered the first Western autobiography, and he is one of the founders of Western theology. He is the theological fountainhead of the Reformation teaching on salvation and grace, and his influence on Christianity is thought by many to be second only to that of Saint Paul.

**Famous Quote:** "Our hearts were made for You, O Lord, and they are restless until they rest in You."

**Famous Works:** *Confessions, Handbook on Faith, Hope, and Love, On Christian Doctrine, The City of God, On the Trinity, Enchiridion*

**Died:** August 28, 430, in Hippo Regius (now Algeria) during a siege of Hippo by the Vandals.

**Conversion Experience:** After a wild youth and conversion to Manichaeism in the summer of 386, Augustine read an account of the life of Saint Anthony of the Desert, which greatly inspired him. Subsequently, he underwent a profound personal crisis and converted to Christianity. He was baptized on Easter of 387, abandoned his career in rhetoric, quit his teaching position in Milan, gave up any ideas of marriage, and devoted himself entirely to serving God and the practices of priesthood, which included celibacy.

**Miscellaneous Facts:** Augustine was canonized by popular recognition and recognized as a Doctor of the Church.

He is considered the patron saint of brewers, printers, theologians, sore eyes, and a number of cities and dioceses.

# CHAPTER I.

---

## The Occasion and Purpose of This "Manual"

1. I cannot say, my dearest son Laurence, how much your learning pleases me, and how much I desire that you should be wise—though not one of those of whom it is said: "Where is the wise? Where is the scribe? Where is the disputant of this world? Hath not God made foolish the wisdom of this world?"[1] Rather, you should be one of those of whom it is written, "The multitude of the wise is the health of the world"[2]; and also you should be the kind of man the apostle wishes those men to be to whom he said,[3] "I would have you be wise in goodness and simple in evil."[4]

2. Human wisdom consists in piety. This you have in the book of the saintly Job, for there he writes that Wisdom herself said to man, "Behold, piety is wisdom."[5] If, then, you ask what kind of piety she was speaking of, you will find it more distinctly designated by the Greek term *theosebeia*, literally, "the service of God." The Greek has still another word for "piety," *ensebeia*, which also signifies "proper service." This too refers chiefly to the

1

service of God. But no term is better than *theosebeia*, which clearly expresses the idea of the man's service of God as the source of human wisdom.

When you ask me to be brief, you do not expect me to speak of great issues in a few sentences, do you? Is not this rather what you desire: a brief summary or a short treatise on the proper mode of worshipping [serving] God?

3. If I should answer, "God should be worshipped in faith, hope, love," you would doubtless reply that this was shorter than you wished, and might then beg for a brief explication of what each of these three means: What should be believed, what should be hoped for, and what should be loved? If I should answer these questions, you would then have everything you asked for in your letter. If you have kept a copy of it, you can easily refer to it. If not, recall your questions as I discuss them.

4. It is your desire, as you wrote, to have from me a book, a sort of *enchiridion*,[6] as it might be called—something to have "at hand"—that deals with your questions. What is to be sought after above all else? What, in view of the divers heresies, is to be avoided above all else? How far does reason support religion; or what happens to reason when the issues involved concern faith alone; what is the beginning and end of our endeavor? What is

the most comprehensive of all explanations? What is the certain and distinctive foundation of the catholic faith? You would have the answers to all these questions if you really understood what a man should believe, what he should hope for, and what he ought to love. For these are the chief things—indeed, the only things—to seek for in religion. He who turns away from them is either a complete stranger to the name of Christ or else he is a heretic. Things that arise in sensory experience, or that are analyzed by the intellect, may be demonstrated by the reason. But in matters that pass beyond the scope of the physical senses, which we have not settled by our own understanding, and cannot—here we must believe, without hesitation, the witness of those men by whom the Scriptures (rightly called divine) were composed, men who were divinely aided in their senses and their minds to see and even to foresee the things about which they testify.

5. But, as this faith, which works by love,[7] begins to penetrate the soul, it tends, through the vital power of goodness, to change into sight, so that the holy and perfect in heart catch glimpses of that ineffable beauty whose full vision is our highest happiness. Here, then, surely, is the answer to your question about the beginning and the end of our endeavor. We begin in faith, we are perfected in sight.[8] This likewise is the most comprehensive of all explanations. As for the

certain and distinctive foundation of the catholic faith, it is Christ. "For other foundation," said the apostle, "can no man lay save that which has been laid, which is Christ Jesus."[9] Nor should it be denied that this is the distinctive basis of the catholic faith, just because it appears that it is common to us and to certain heretics as well. For if we think carefully about the meaning of Christ, we shall see that among some of the heretics who wish to be called Christians, the *name* of Christ is held in honor, but the reality itself is not among them. To make all this plain would take too long—because we would then have to review all the heresies that have been, the ones that now exist, and those which could exist under the label "Christian," and we would have to show that what we have said of all is true of each of them. Such a discussion would take so many volumes as to make it seem endless.[10]

6. You have asked for an *enchiridion*, something you could carry around, not just baggage for your bookshelf. Therefore we may return to these three ways in which, as we said, God should be served: faith, hope, love. It is easy to say what one ought to believe, what to hope for, and what to love. But to defend our doctrines against the calumnies of those who think differently is a more difficult and detailed task. If one is to have this wisdom, it is not enough just to put an *enchiridion* in the hand. It is also necessary that a great zeal be kindled in the heart.

# CHAPTER II.

## The Creed and the Lord's Prayer as Guides to the Interpretation of the Theological Virtues of Faith, Hope, and Love

7. Let us begin, for example, with the Symbol[11] and the Lord's Prayer. What is shorter to hear or to read? What is more easily memorized? Since through sin the human race stood grievously burdened by great misery and in deep need of mercy, a prophet, preaching of the time of God's grace, said, "And it shall be that all who invoke the Lord's name will be saved."[12] Thus, we have the Lord's Prayer. Later, the apostle, when he wished to commend this same grace, remembered this prophetic testimony and promptly added, "But how shall they invoke him in whom they have not believed?"[13] Thus, we have the Symbol. In these two we have the three theological virtues working together: faith believes; hope and love pray. Yet without faith nothing else is possible; thus faith prays too. This, then, is the meaning of the saying, "How shall they invoke him in whom they have not believed?"

8. Now, is it possible to hope for what we do not believe in? We can, of course, believe in something that we do not hope for. Who among the faithful does not believe in the punishment of the impious? Yet he does not hope for it, and whoever believes that such a punishment is threatening him and draws back in horror from it is more rightly said to fear than to hope. A poet, distinguishing between these two feelings, said,

"*Let those who dread be allowed to hope,*"[14]

but another poet, and a better one, did not put it rightly:

"*Here, if I could have hoped for [i.e., foreseen] such a grievous blow ...*"[15]

Indeed, some grammarians use this as an example of inaccurate language and comment, "He said 'to hope' when he should have said 'to fear.'"

Therefore faith may refer to evil things as well as to good, since we believe in both the good and evil. Yet faith is good, not evil. Moreover, faith refers to things past and present and future. For we believe that Christ died; this is a past event. We believe that he sitteth at the Father's right hand; this is present. We believe that he will come as our judge; this is future. Again, faith has to do with our own affairs and with those of others. For everyone believes, both about himself and other persons—and about things as well—that at some time he began to exist and that he has not existed forever. Thus, not only about men, but even about angels, we believe many things that have a bearing on religion.

But hope deals only with good things, and only with those which lie in the future, and which pertain to the man who cherishes the hope. Since this is so, faith must be distinguished from hope: they are different terms and likewise different concepts. Yet faith and hope have this in common: they refer to what is not seen, whether this unseen is believed in or hoped for. Thus in the Epistle to the Hebrews, which is used by the enlightened defenders of the catholic rule of faith, faith is said to be "the conviction of things not seen."[16] However, when a man maintains that neither words nor witnesses nor even arguments, but only the evidence of present experience, determine his faith, he still ought not to be called absurd or told, "You have seen; therefore you have not believed." For it does not follow that unless a thing is not seen it cannot be believed. Still it is better for us to use the term "faith," as we are taught in "the sacred eloquence,"[17] to refer to things not seen. And as for hope, the apostle says: "Hope that is seen is not hope. For if a man sees a thing, why does he hope for it? If, however, we hope for what we do not see, we then wait for it in patience."[18] When, therefore, our good is believed to be future, this is the same thing as hoping for it.

What, then, shall I say of love, without which faith can do nothing? There can be no true hope without love. Indeed, as the apostle James says, "Even the demons believe and tremble."[19]

Yet they neither hope nor love. Instead, believing as we do that what we hope for and love is coming to pass, they tremble. Therefore, the apostle Paul approves and commends the faith that works by love and that cannot exist without hope. Thus it is that love is not without hope, hope is not without love, and neither hope nor love are without faith.

# CHAPTER III.

## God the Creator of All; and the Goodness of All Creation

9. Wherefore, when it is asked what we ought to believe in matters of religion, the answer is not to be sought in the exploration of the nature of things [*rerum natura*], after the manner of those whom the Greeks called "physicists."[20] Nor should we be dismayed if Christians are ignorant about the properties and the number of the basic elements of nature, or about the motion, order, and deviations of the stars, the map of the heavens, the kinds and nature of animals, plants, stones, springs, rivers, and mountains; about the divisions of space and time, about the signs of impending storms, and the myriad other things which these "physicists" have come to understand, or think they have. For even these men, gifted with such superior insight, with their ardor in study and their abundant leisure, exploring some of these matters by human conjecture and others through historical inquiry, have not yet learned everything there is to know. For that matter, many of the things they are so proud to have discovered are more often matters of opinion than of verified knowledge.

For the Christian, it is enough to believe that the cause of all created things, whether in heaven or on earth, whether visible or invisible, is nothing other than the goodness of the Creator, who is the one and the true God.[21] Further, the Christian believes that nothing exists save God himself and what comes from him; and he believes that God is triune, i.e., the Father, and the Son begotten of the Father, and the Holy Spirit proceeding from the same Father, but one and the same Spirit of the Father and the Son.

10. By this Trinity, supremely and equally and immutably good, were all things created. But they were not created supremely, equally, nor immutably good. Still, each single created thing is good, and taken as a whole they are very good, because together they constitute a universe of admirable beauty.

11. In this universe, even what is called evil, when it is rightly ordered and kept in its place, commends the good more eminently, since good things yield greater pleasure and praise when compared to the bad things. For the Omnipotent God, whom even the heathen acknowledge as the Supreme Power over all, would not allow any evil in his works, unless in his omnipotence and goodness, as the Supreme Good, he is able to bring forth good out of evil. What, after all, is anything we call evil except the privation of good? In animal bodies,

for instance, sickness and wounds are nothing but the privation of health. When a cure is effected, the evils which were present (i.e., the sickness and the wounds) do not retreat and go elsewhere. Rather, they simply do not exist any more. For such evil is not a substance; the wound or the disease is a defect of the bodily substance which, as a substance, is good. Evil, then, is an accident, i.e., a privation of that good which is called health. Thus, whatever defects there are in a soul are privations of a natural good. When a cure takes place, they are not transferred elsewhere but, since they are no longer present in the state of health, they no longer exist at all.[22]

# CHAPTER IV.

## The Problem of Evil

12. All of nature, therefore, is good, since the Creator of all nature is supremely good. But nature is not supremely and immutably good as is the Creator of it. Thus the good in created things can be diminished and augmented. For good to be diminished is evil; still, however much it is diminished, something must remain of its original nature as long as it exists at all. For no matter what kind or however insignificant a thing may be, the good which is its "nature" cannot be destroyed without the thing itself being destroyed. There is good reason, therefore, to praise an uncorrupted thing, and if it were indeed an incorruptible thing which could not be destroyed, it would doubtless be all the more worthy of praise. When, however, a thing is corrupted, its corruption is an evil because it is, by just so much, a privation of the good. Where there is no privation of the good, there is no evil. Where there is evil, there is a corresponding diminution of the good. As long, then, as a thing is being corrupted, there is good in it of which it is being deprived; and in this process, if something of its being remains that cannot be further corrupted, this

will then be an incorruptible entity [*natura incorruptibilis*], and to this great good it will have come through the process of corruption. But even if the corruption is not arrested, it still does not cease having some good of which it cannot be further deprived. If, however, the corruption comes to be total and entire, there is no good left either, because it is no longer an entity at all. Wherefore corruption cannot consume the good without also consuming the thing itself. Every actual entity [*natura*] is therefore good; a greater good if it cannot be corrupted, a lesser good if it can be. Yet only the foolish and unknowing can deny that it is still good even when corrupted. Whenever a thing is consumed by corruption, not even the corruption remains, for it is nothing in itself, having no subsistent being in which to exist.

13. From this it follows that there is nothing to be called evil if there is nothing good. A good that wholly lacks an evil aspect is entirely good. Where there is some evil in a thing, its good is defective or defectible. Thus there can be no evil where there is no good. This leads us to a surprising conclusion: that, since every being, in so far as it is a being, is good, if we then say that a defective thing is bad, it would seem to mean that we are saying that what is evil is good, that only what is good is ever evil and that there is no evil apart from something good. This is because every actual entity is good [*omnis natura*

*bonum est.*] Nothing evil exists *in itself*, but only as an evil aspect of some actual entity. Therefore, there can be nothing evil except something good. Absurd as this sounds, nevertheless the logical connections of the argument compel us to it as inevitable. At the same time, we must take warning lest we incur the prophetic judgment which reads: "Woe to those who call evil good and good evil: who call darkness light and light darkness; who call the bitter sweet and the sweet bitter."[23] Moreover the Lord himself saith: "An evil man brings forth evil out of the evil treasure of his heart."[24] What, then, is an evil man but an evil entity [*natura mala*], since man is an entity? Now, if a man is something good because he is an entity, what, then, is a bad man except an evil good? When, however, we distinguish between these two concepts, we find that the bad man is not bad because he is a man, nor is he good because he is wicked. Rather, he is a good entity in so far as he is a man, evil in so far as he is wicked. Therefore, if anyone says that simply to be a man is evil, or that to be a wicked man is good, he rightly falls under the prophetic judgment: "Woe to him who calls evil good and good evil." For this amounts to finding fault with God's work, because man is an entity of God's creation. It also means that we are praising the defects in this particular man *because* he is a wicked person. Thus, every entity, even if it is a defective one, in so far as it is an entity, is good. In so far as it is defective, it is evil.

14. Actually, then, in these two contraries we call evil and good, the rule of the logicians fails to apply.[25] No weather is both dark and bright at the same time; no food or drink is both sweet and sour at the same time; no body is, at the same time and place, both white and black, nor deformed and well-formed at the same time. This principle is found to apply in almost all disjunctions: two contraries cannot coexist in a single thing. Nevertheless, while no one maintains that good and evil are not contraries, they can not only coexist, but the evil cannot exist at all without the good, or in a thing that is not a good. On the other hand, the good can exist without evil. For a man or an angel could exist and yet not be wicked, whereas there cannot be wickedness except in a man or an angel. It is good to be a man, good to be an angel; but evil to be wicked. These two contraries are thus coexistent, so that if there were no good in what is evil, then the evil simply could not be, since it can have no mode in which to exist, nor any source from which corruption springs, unless it be something corruptible. Unless this something is good, it cannot be corrupted, because corruption is nothing more than the deprivation of the good. Evils, therefore, have their source in the good, and unless they are parasitic on something good, they are not anything at all. There is no other source whence an evil thing can come to be. If this is the case, then, in so far as a thing is an entity, it is unquestionably good. If it is an incorruptible entity,

it is a great good. But even if it is a corruptible entity, it still has no mode of existence except as an aspect of something that is good. Only by corrupting something good can corruption inflict injury.

15. But when we say that evil has its source in the good, do not suppose that this denies our Lord's judgment: "A good tree cannot bear evil fruit."[26] This cannot be, even as the Truth himself declareth: "Men do not gather grapes from thorns," since thorns cannot bear grapes. Nevertheless, from good soil we can see both vines and thorns spring up. Likewise, just as a bad tree does not grow good fruit, so also an evil will does not produce good deeds. From a human nature, which is good in itself, there can spring forth either a good or an evil will. There was no other place from whence evil could have arisen in the first place except from the nature—good in itself—of an angel or a man. This is what our Lord himself most clearly shows in the passage about the trees and the fruits, for he said: "Make the tree good and the fruits will be good, or make the tree bad and its fruits will be bad."[27] This is warning enough that bad fruit cannot grow on a good tree nor good fruit on a bad one. Yet from that same earth to which he was referring, both sorts of trees can grow.

# CHAPTER V.

## The Kinds and Degrees of Error

16. This being the case, when that verse of Maro's gives us pleasure,

*"Happy is he who can understand the causes of things,"*[28]

it still does not follow that our felicity depends upon our knowing the causes of the great physical processes in the world, which are hidden in the secret maze of nature,

*"Whence earthquakes, whose force swells the sea to flood, so that they burst their bounds and then subside again,"*[29]

and other such things as this.

But we ought to know the causes of good and evil in things, at least as far as men may do so in this life, filled as it is with errors and distress, in order to avoid these errors and distresses. We must always aim at that true felicity wherein misery does not distract, nor error mislead. If it is a good thing to understand the causes of physical motion, there is nothing of greater concern in these matters which we ought to understand than our own health. But when we are in ignorance of such things, we seek out a physician, who has seen how the secrets of heaven and earth still remain hidden from us, and what patience there must be in unknowing.

17. Although we should beware of error wherever possible, not only in great matters but in small ones as well, it is impossible not to be ignorant of many things. Yet it does not follow that one falls into error out of ignorance alone. If someone thinks he knows what he does not know, if he approves as true what is actually false, this then is error, in the proper sense of the term. Obviously, much depends on the question involved in the error, for in one and the same question one naturally prefers the instructed to the ignorant, the expert to the blunderer, and this with good reason. In a complex issue, however, as when one man knows one thing and another man knows something else, if the former knowledge is more useful and the latter is less useful or even harmful, who in this latter case would not prefer ignorance? There are some things, after all, that it is better not to know than to know. Likewise, there is sometimes profit in error—but on a journey, not in morals.[30] This sort of thing happened to us once, when we mistook the way at a crossroads and did not go by the place where an armed gang of Donatists lay in wait to ambush us. We finally arrived at the place where we were going, but only by a

roundabout way, and upon learning of the ambush, we were glad to have erred and gave thanks to God for our error. Who would doubt, in such a situation, that the erring traveler is better off than the unerring brigand? This perhaps explains the meaning of our finest poet, when he speaks for an unhappy lover:

*"When I saw [her] I was undone, and fatal error swept me away,"*[31]

for there is such a thing as a fortunate mistake which not only does no harm but actually does some good.

But now for a more careful consideration of the truth in this business. To err means nothing more than to judge as true what is in fact false, and as false what is true. It means to be certain about the uncertain, uncertain about the certain, whether it be certainly true or certainly false. This sort of error in the mind is deforming and improper, since the fitting and proper thing would be to be able to say, in speech or judgment: "Yes, yes. No, no."[32] Actually, the wretched lives we lead come partly from this: that sometimes if they are not to be entirely lost, error is unavoidable. It is different in that higher life where Truth itself is the life of our souls, where none deceives and none is deceived. In this life men deceive and are deceived, and are actually worse off when they deceive by lying than when they are deceived by believing lies. Yet our rational mind shrinks from falsehood, and naturally avoids error as much as it can, so that even a deceiver is unwilling to be deceived by somebody else.[33] For the liar thinks he does not deceive himself and that he deceives only those who believe him. Indeed, he does not err in his lying, if he himself knows what the truth is. But he is deceived in this, that he supposes that his lie does no harm to himself, when actually every sin harms the one who commits it more that it does the one who suffers it.

# CHAPTER VI.

## The Problem of Lying

18. Here a most difficult and complex issue arises which I once dealt with in a large book, in response to the urgent question whether it is ever the duty of a righteous man to lie.[34] Some go so far as to contend that in cases concerning the worship of God or even the nature of God, it is sometimes a good and pious deed to speak falsely. It seems to me, however, that every lie is a sin, albeit there is a great difference depending on the intention and the topic of the lie. He does not sin as much who lies in the attempt to be helpful as the man who lies as a part of a deliberate wickedness. Nor does one who, by lying, sets a traveler on the wrong road do as much harm as one who, by a deceitful lie, perverts the way of a life. Obviously, no one should be adjudged a liar who speaks falsely what he sincerely supposes is the truth, since in his case he does not deceive but rather is deceived. Likewise, a man is not a liar, though he could be charged with rashness, when he incautiously accepts as true what is false. On the other hand, however, that man is a liar in his own conscience who speaks the truth supposing that it is a falsehood. For as far as his soul is

concerned, since he did not say what he believed, he did not tell the truth, even though the truth did come out in what he said. Nor is a man to be cleared of the charge of lying whose mouth unknowingly speaks the truth while his conscious intention is to lie. If we do not consider the things spoken of, but only the intentions of the one speaking, he is the better man who unknowingly speaks falsely—because he judges his statement to be true—than the one who unknowingly speaks the truth while in his heart he is attempting to deceive. For the first man does not have one intention in his heart and another in his word, whereas the other, whatever be the facts in his statement, still "has one thought locked in his heart, another ready on his tongue,"[35] which is the very essence of lying. But when we do consider the things spoken of, it makes a great difference in what respect one is deceived or lies. To be deceived is a lesser evil than to lie, as far as a man's intentions are concerned. But it is far more tolerable that a man should lie about things not connected with religion than for one to be deceived in matters where faith and knowledge are prerequisite to the proper service of God. To illustrate what I mean by examples: If one man lies by saying that a dead man is alive, and another man, being deceived, believes that Christ will die again after some extended future period—would it not be incomparably better to lie in the first case than to be deceived in the second? And would it not be a lesser evil to lead someone into the former error than to be led by someone into the latter?

19. In some things, then, we are deceived in great matters; in others, small. In some of them no harm is done; in others, even good results. It is a great evil for a man to be deceived so as not to believe what would lead him to life eternal, or what would lead to eternal death. But it is a small evil to be deceived by crediting a falsehood as the truth in a matter where one brings on himself some temporal setback which can then be turned to good use by being borne in faithful patience—as for example, when someone judges a man to be good who is actually bad, and consequently has to suffer evil on his account. Or, take the man who believes a bad man to be good, yet suffers no harm at his hand. He is not badly deceived nor would the prophetic condemnation fall on him: "Woe to those who call evil good." For we should understand that this saying refers to the things in which men are evil and not to the men themselves. Hence, he who calls adultery a good thing may be rightly accused by the prophetic word. But if he calls a man good supposing him to be chaste and not knowing that he is an adulterer, such a man is not deceived in his doctrine of good and evil, but only as to the secrets of human conduct. He calls the man good on the basis of what he supposed him to be, and this is undoubtedly a good thing. Moreover, he calls adultery bad and chastity good. But

he calls this particular man good in ignorance of the fact that he is an adulterer and not chaste. In similar fashion, if one escapes an injury through an error, as I mentioned before happened to me on that journey, there is even something good that accrues to a man through his mistakes. But when I say that in such a case a man may be deceived without suffering harm therefrom, or even may gain some benefit thereby, I am not saying that error is not a bad thing, nor that it is a positively good thing. I speak only of the evil which did not happen or the good which did happen, through the error, which was not caused by the error itself but which came out of it. Error, in itself and by itself, whether a great error in great matters or a small error in small affairs, is always a bad thing. For who, except in error, denies that it is bad to approve the false as though it were the truth, or to disapprove the truth as though it were falsehood, or to hold what is certain as if it were uncertain, or what is uncertain as if it were certain? It is one thing to judge a man good who is actually bad—this is an error. It is quite another thing not to suffer harm from something evil if the wicked man whom we supposed to be good actually does nothing harmful to us. It is one thing to suppose that this particular road is the right one when it is not. It is quite another thing that, from this error—which is a bad thing—something good actually turns out, such as being saved from the onslaught of wicked men.

# CHAPTER VII.

## Disputed Questions about the Limits of Knowledge and Certainty in Various Matters

20. I do not rightly know whether errors of this sort should be called sins—when one thinks well of a wicked man, not knowing what his character really is, or when, instead of our physical perception, similar perceptions occur which we experience in the spirit (such as the illusion of the apostle Peter when he thought he was seeing a vision but was actually being liberated from fetters and chains by the angel[36] Or in perceptual illusions when we think something is smooth which is actually rough, or something sweet which is bitter, something fragrant which is putrid, that a noise is thunder when it is actually a wagon passing by, when one takes this man for that, or when two men look alike, as happens in the case of twins—whence our poet speaks of "a pleasant error for parents"[37]—say I do not know whether these and other such errors should be called sins.

Nor am I at the moment trying to deal with that knottiest of questions which baffled the most acute men of the Academy, whether a wise man ought ever to affirm anything positively lest he be involved in the error of affirming as true what may be false, since all questions, as they assert, are either mysterious [*occulta*] or uncertain. On these points I wrote three books in the early stages of my conversion because my further progress was being blocked by objections like this which stood at the very threshold of my understanding.[38] It was necessary to overcome the despair of being unable to attain to truth, which is what their arguments seemed to lead one to. Among them every error is deemed a sin, and this can be warded off only by a systematic suspension of positive assent. Indeed they say it is an error if someone believes in what is uncertain. For them, however, nothing is certain in human experience, because of the deceitful likeness of falsehood to the truth, so that even if what appears to be true turns out to be true indeed, they will still dispute it with the most acute and even shameless arguments.

Among us, on the other hand, "the righteous man lives by faith."[39] Now, if you take away positive affirmation,[40] you take away faith, for without positive affirmation nothing is believed. And there are truths about things unseen, and unless they are believed, we cannot attain to the happy life, which is nothing less than life eternal. It is a question whether we ought to argue with those who profess themselves ignorant not only about the eternity yet to come but also about their present existence, for they [the Academics] even argue that they do not know what they cannot help knowing. For no one can "not know" that he himself is alive. If he is not alive, he cannot "not know" about it or anything else at all, because either to know or to "not know" implies a living subject. But, in such a case, by not positively affirming that they are alive, the skeptics ward off the appearance of error in themselves, yet they do make errors simply by showing themselves alive; one cannot err who is not alive. That we live is therefore not only true, but it is altogether certain as well. And there are many things that are thus true and certain concerning which, if we withhold positive assent, this ought not to be regarded as a higher wisdom but actually a sort of dementia.

21. In those things which do not concern our attainment of the Kingdom of God, it does not matter whether they are believed in or not, or whether they are true or are supposed to be true or false. To err in such questions, to mistake one thing for another, is not to be judged as a sin or, if it is, as a small and light one. In sum, whatever kind or how much of an error these miscues may be, it does not involve the way that leads to God, which is the faith of Christ which works through love. This way of life was not abandoned in that error so dear to parents concerning the twins.[41] Nor did the apostle

Peter deviate from this way when he thought he saw a vision and so mistook one thing for something else. In his case, he did not discover the actual situation until after the angel, by whom he was freed, had departed from him. Nor did the patriarch Jacob deviate from this way when he believed that his son, who was in fact alive, had been devoured by a wild beast. We may err through false impressions of this kind, with our faith in God still safe, nor do we thus leave the way that leads us to him. Nevertheless, such mistakes, even if they are not sins, must still be listed among the evils of this life, which is so readily subject to vanity that we judge the false for true, reject the true for the false, and hold as uncertain what is actually certain. For even if these mistakes do not affect that faith by which we move forward to affirm truth and eternal beatitude, yet they are not unrelated to the misery in which we still exist. Actually, of course, we would be deceived in nothing at all, either in our souls or our physical senses, if we were already enjoying that true and perfected happiness.

22. Every lie, then, must be called a sin, because every man ought to speak what is in his heart—not only when he himself knows the truth, but even when he errs and is deceived, as a man may be. This is so whether it be true or is only supposed to be true when it is not. But a man who lies says the opposite of what is in his heart, with the deliberate intent to deceive. Now clearly,

language, in its proper function, was developed not as a means whereby men could deceive one another, but as a medium through which a man could communicate his thought to others. Wherefore to use language in order to deceive, and not as it was designed to be used, is a sin.

Nor should we suppose that there is any such thing as a lie that is not a sin, just because we suppose that we can sometimes help somebody by lying. For we could also do this by stealing, as when a secret theft from a rich man who does not feel the loss is openly given to a pauper who greatly appreciates the gain. Yet no one would say that such a theft was not a sin. Or again, we could also "help" by committing adultery, if someone appeared to be dying for love if we would not consent to her desire and who, if she lived, might be purified by repentance. But it cannot be denied that such an adultery would be a sin. If, then, we hold chastity in such high regard, wherein has truth offended us so that although chastity must not be violated by adultery, even for the sake of some other good, yet truth may be violated by lying? That men have made progress toward the good, when they will not lie save for the sake of human values, is not to be denied. But what is rightly praised in such a forward step, and perhaps even rewarded, is their good will and not their deceit. The deceit may be pardoned, but certainly ought not to be praised, especially among the heirs of the New Covenant to whom it has been said, "Let your speech be yes, yes; no, no: for what is more than this comes from evil."[42] Yet because of what this evil does, never ceasing to subvert this mortality of ours, even the joint heirs of Christ themselves pray, "Forgive us our debts."[43]

# CHAPTER VIII.

## The Plight of Man After the Fall

23. With this much said, within the necessary brevity of this kind of treatise, as to what we need to know about the causes of good and evil—enough to lead us in the way toward the Kingdom, where there will be life without death, truth without error, happiness without anxiety—we ought not to doubt in any way that the cause of everything pertaining to our good is nothing other than the bountiful goodness of God himself. The cause of evil is the defection of the will of a being who is mutably good from the Good which is immutable. This happened first in the case of the angels and, afterward, that of man.

24. This was the primal lapse of the rational creature, that is, his first privation of the good. In train of this there crept in, even without his willing it, ignorance of the right things to do and also an appetite for noxious things. And these brought along with them, as their companions, error and misery. When these two evils are felt to be imminent, the soul's motion in flight from them is called fear. Moreover, as the soul's appetites are

satisfied by things harmful or at least inane—and as it fails to recognize the error of its ways—it falls victim to unwholesome pleasures or may even be exhilarated by vain joys. From these tainted springs of action—moved by the lash of appetite rather than a feeling of plenty—there flows out every kind of misery which is now the lot of rational natures.

25. Yet such a nature, even in its evil state, could not lose its appetite for blessedness. There are the evils that both men and angels have in common, for whose wickedness God hath condemned them in simple justice. But man has a unique penalty as well: he is also punished by the death of the body. God had indeed threatened man with death as penalty if he should sin. He endowed him with freedom of the will in order that he might rule him by rational command and deter him by the threat of death. He even placed him in the happiness of paradise in a sheltered nook of life [*in umbra vitae*] where, by being a good steward of righteousness, he would rise to better things.

26. From this state, after he had sinned, man was banished, and through his sin he subjected his descendants to the punishment of sin and damnation, for he had radically corrupted them, in himself, by his sinning. As a consequence of this, all those descended from him and his wife (who had prompted him to sin and who was

condemned along with him at the same time)—all those born through carnal lust, on whom the same penalty is visited as for disobedience—all these entered into the inheritance of original sin. Through this involvement they were led, through divers errors and sufferings (along with the rebel angels, their corruptors and possessors and companions), to that final stage of punishment without end. "Thus by one man, sin entered into the world and death through sin; and thus death came upon all men, since all men have sinned."[44] By "the world" in this passage the apostle is, of course, referring to the whole human race.

27. This, then, was the situation: the whole mass of the human race stood condemned, lying ruined and wallowing in evil, being plunged from evil into evil and, having joined causes with the angels who had sinned, it was paying the fully deserved penalty for impious desertion. Certainly the anger of God rests, in full justice, on the deeds that the wicked do freely in blind and unbridled lust; and it is manifest in whatever penalties they are called on to suffer, both openly and secretly. Yet the Creator's goodness does not cease to sustain life and vitality even in the evil angels, for were *this* sustenance withdrawn, they would simply cease to exist. As for mankind, although born of a corrupted and condemned stock, he still retains the power to form and animate his seed, to direct his members in their tempo-

ral order, to enliven his senses in their spatial relations, and to provide bodily nourishment. For God judged it better to bring good out of evil than not to permit any evil to exist. And if he had willed that there should be no reformation in the case of men, as there is none for the wicked angels, would it not have been just if the nature that deserted God and, through the evil use of his powers, trampled and transgressed the precepts of his Creator, which could have been easily kept—the same creature who stubbornly turned away from His Light and violated the image of the Creator in himself, who had in the evil use of his free will broken away from the wholesome discipline of God's law—would it not have been just if such a being had been abandoned by God wholly and forever and laid under the everlasting punishment which he deserved? Clearly God would have done this if he were only just and not also merciful and if he had not willed to show far more striking evidence of his mercy by pardoning some who were unworthy of it.

# CHAPTER IX.

## The Replacement of the Fallen Angels by Elect Men; The Necessity of Grace

28. While some of the angels deserted God in impious pride and were cast into the lowest darkness from the brightness of their heavenly home, the remaining number of the angels persevered in eternal bliss and holiness with God. For these faithful angels were not descended from a single angel, lapsed and damned. Hence, the original evil did not bind them in the fetters of inherited guilt, nor did it hand the whole company over to a deserved punishment, as is the human lot. Instead, when he who became the devil first rose in rebellion with his impious company and was then with them prostrated, the rest of the angels stood fast in pious obedience to the Lord and so received what the others had not had—a sure knowledge of their everlasting security in his unfailing steadfastness.

29. Thus it pleased God, Creator and Governor of the universe, that since the whole multitude of the angels had not perished in this desertion of him, those who had perished would remain forever in perdition,

but those who had remained loyal through the revolt should go on rejoicing in the certain knowledge of the bliss forever theirs. From the other part of the rational creation—that is, mankind—although it had perished as a whole through sins and punishments, both original and personal, God had determined that a portion of it would be restored and would fill up the loss which that diabolical disaster had caused in the angelic society. For this is the promise to the saints at the resurrection, that they shall be equal to the angels of God.[45]

Thus the heavenly Jerusalem, our mother and the commonwealth of God, shall not be defrauded of her full quota of citizens, but perhaps will rule over an even larger number. We know neither the number of holy men nor of the filthy demons, whose places are to be filled by the sons of the holy mother, who seemed barren in the earth, but whose sons will abide time without end in the peace the demons lost. But the number of those citizens, whether those who now belong or those who will in the future, is known to the mind of the Maker, "who calleth into existence things which are not, as though they were,"[46] and "ordereth all things in measure and number and weight."[47]

30. But now, can that part of the human race to whom God hath promised deliverance and a place in the eternal Kingdom be restored through the merits of their own

works? Of course not! For what good works could a lost soul do except as he had been rescued from his lostness? Could he do this by the determination of his free will? Of course not! For it was in the evil use of his free will that man destroyed himself and his will at the same time. For as a man who kills himself is still alive when he kills himself, but having killed himself is then no longer alive and cannot resuscitate himself after he has destroyed his own life—so also sin which arises from the action of the free will turns out to be victor over the will and the free will is destroyed. "By whom a man is overcome, to this one he then is bound as slave."[48] This is clearly the judgment of the apostle Peter. And since it is true, I ask you what kind of liberty can one have who is bound as a slave except the liberty that loves to sin?

He serves freely who freely does the will of his master. Accordingly he who is slave to sin is free to sin. But thereafter he will not be free to do right unless he is delivered from the bondage of sin and begins to be the servant of righteousness. This, then, is true liberty: the joy that comes in doing what is right. At the same time, it is also devoted service in obedience to righteous precept.

But how would a man, bound and sold, get back his liberty to do good, unless he could regain it from Him whose voice saith, "If the Son shall make you free, then you will be free indeed"[49]? But before this process begins in man, could anyone glory in his good works as if they were acts of his free will, when he is not yet free to act rightly? He could do this only if, puffed up in proud vanity, he were merely boasting. This attitude is what the apostle was reproving when he said, "By grace you have been saved by faith."[50]

31. And lest men should arrogate to themselves saving faith as their own work and not understand it as a divine gift, the same apostle who says somewhere else that he had "obtained mercy of the Lord to be trustworthy"[51] makes here an additional comment: "And this is not of yourselves, rather it is a gift of God—not because of works either, lest any man should boast."[52] But then, lest it be supposed that the faithful are lacking in good works, he added further, "For we are his workmanship, created in Christ Jesus to good works, which God hath prepared beforehand for us to walk in them."[53]

We are then truly free when God ordereth our lives, that is, formeth and createth us not as men—this he hath already done—but also as good men, which he is now doing by his grace, that we may indeed be new creatures in Christ Jesus.[54] Accordingly, the prayer: "Create in me a clean heart, O God."[55] This does not mean, as far as the natural human heart is concerned, that God hath not already created this.

32. Once again, lest anyone glory, if not in his own works, at least in the determination of his free will, as if some merit had originated from him and as if the freedom to do good works had been bestowed on him as a kind of reward, let him hear the same herald of grace, announcing: "For it is God who is at work in you both to will and to do according to his good will."[56] And, in another place: "It is not therefore a matter of man's willing, or of his running, but of God's showing mercy."[57] Still, it is obvious that a man who is old enough to exercise his reason cannot believe, hope, or love unless he wills it, nor could he run for the prize of his high calling in God without a decision of his will. In what sense, therefore, is it "not a matter of human willing or running but of God's showing mercy," unless it be that "the will itself is prepared by the Lord," even as it is written?[58] This saying, therefore, that "it is not a matter of human willing or running but of God's showing mercy," means that the action is from both, that is to say, from the will of man and from the mercy of God. Thus we accept the dictum, "It is not a matter of human willing or running but of God's showing mercy," as if it meant, "The will of man is not sufficient by itself unless there is also the mercy of God." By the same token, the mercy of God is not sufficient by itself unless there is also the will of man. But if we say rightly that "it is not a matter of human willing or running but of God's showing mercy," because the will of man alone is not

enough, why, then, is not the contrary rightly said, "It is not a matter of God's showing mercy but of a man's willing," since the mercy of God by itself alone is not enough? Now, actually, no Christian would dare to say, "It is not a matter of God's showing mercy but of man's willing," lest he explicitly contradict the apostle. The conclusion remains, therefore, that this saying: "Not man's willing or running but God's showing mercy," is to be understood to mean that the whole process is credited to God, who both prepareth the will to receive divine aid and aideth the will which has been thus prepared.[59]

For a man's good will comes before many other gifts from God, but not all of them. One of the gifts it does not antedate is—just itself! Thus in the Sacred Eloquence we read both, "His mercy goes before me,"[60] and also, "His mercy shall follow me."[61] It predisposes a man before he wills, to prompt his willing. It follows the act of willing, lest one's will be frustrated. Otherwise, why are we admonished to pray for our enemies,[62] who are plainly not now willing to live piously, unless it be that God is even now at work in them and in their wills?[63] Or again, why are we admonished to ask in order to receive, unless it be that He who grants us what we will is he through whom it comes to pass that we will? We pray for enemies, therefore, that the mercy of God should go before them, as it goes before us; we pray for

42

ourselves that his mercy shall follow us.

# CHAPTER X.

## Jesus Christ the Mediator

33. Thus it was that the human race was bound in a just doom and all men were children of wrath. Of this wrath it is written: "For all our days are wasted; we are ruined in thy wrath; our years seem like a spider's web."[64] Likewise Job spoke of this wrath: "Man born of woman is of few days and full of trouble."[65] And even the Lord Jesus said of it: "He that believes in the Son has life everlasting, but he that believes not does not have life. Instead, the wrath of God abides in him."[66] He does not say, "It will come," but, "It now abides." Indeed every man is born into this state. Wherefore the apostle says, "For we too were by nature children of wrath even as the others."[67] Since men are in this state of wrath through original sin—a condition made still graver and more pernicious as they compounded more and worse sins with it—a Mediator was required; that is to say, a Reconciler who by offering a unique sacrifice, of which all the sacrifices of the Law and the Prophets were shadows, should allay that wrath. Thus the apostle says, "For if, when we were enemies, we were reconciled to God by the death of his Son, even more now

being reconciled by his blood we shall be saved from wrath through him."[68] However, when God is said to be wrathful, this does not signify any such perturbation in him as there is in the soul of a wrathful man. His verdict, which is always just, takes the name "wrath" as a term borrowed from the language of human feelings. This, then, is the grace of God through Jesus Christ our Lord—that we are reconciled to God through the Mediator and receive the Holy Spirit so that we may be changed from enemies into sons, "for as many as are led by the Spirit of God, they are the sons of God."[69]

34. It would take too long to say all that would be truly worthy of this Mediator. Indeed, men cannot speak properly of such matters. For who can unfold in cogent enough fashion this statement, that "the Word became flesh and dwelt among us,"[70] so that we should then believe in "the only Son of God the Father Almighty, born of the Holy Spirit and Mary the Virgin." Yet it is indeed true that the Word was made flesh, the flesh being assumed by the Divinity, not the Divinity being changed into flesh. Of course, by the term "flesh" we ought here to understand "man," an expression in which the part signifies the whole, just as it is said, "Since by the works of the law no flesh shall be justified,"[71] which is to say, no *man* shall be justified. Yet certainly we must say that in that assumption nothing was lacking that belongs to human nature.

But it was a nature entirely free from the bonds of all sin. It was not a nature born of both sexes with fleshly desires, with the burden of sin, the guilt of which is washed away in regeneration. Instead, it was the kind of nature that would be fittingly born of a virgin, conceived by His mother's faith and not her fleshly desires. Now if in his being born, her virginity had been destroyed, he would not then have been born of a virgin. It would then be false (which is unthinkable) for the whole Church to confess him "born of the Virgin Mary." This is the Church which, imitating his mother, daily gives birth to his members yet remains virgin. Read, if you please, my letter on the virginity of Saint Mary written to that illustrious man, Volusianus, whom I name with honor and affection.[72]

35. Christ Jesus, Son of God, is thus both God and man. He was God before all ages; he is man in this age of ours. He is God because he is the Word of God, for "the Word was God."[73] Yet he is man also, since in the unity of his Person a rational soul and body is joined to the Word.

Accordingly, in so far as he is God, he and the Father are one. Yet in so far as he is man, the Father is greater than he. Since he was God's only Son—not by grace but by nature—to the end that he might indeed be the fullness of all grace, he was also made Son of Man—and yet he was in the one nature as well as in the other, one Christ. "For being in the form of God, he judged it not a violation to be what he was by nature, the equal of God. Yet he emptied himself, taking on the form of a servant,"[74] yet neither losing nor diminishing the form of God.[75] Thus he was made less and remained equal, and both these in a unity as we said before. But he is one of these because he is the Word; the other, because he was a man. As the Word, he is the equal of the Father; as a man, he is less. He is the one Son of God, and at the same time Son of Man; the one Son of Man, and at the same time God's Son. These are not two sons of God, one God and the other man, but *one* Son of God—God without origin, man with a definite origin—our Lord Jesus Christ.

# CHAPTER XI.

## The Incarnation as Prime Example of the Action of God's Grace

36. In this the grace of God is supremely manifest, commended in grand and visible fashion; for what had the human nature in the man Christ merited, that it, and no other, should be assumed into the unity of the Person of the only Son of God? What good will, what zealous strivings, what good works preceded this assumption by which that particular man deserved to become one Person with God? Was he a man before the union, and was this singular grace given him as to one particularly deserving before God? Of course not! For, from the moment he began to be a man, that man began to be nothing other than God's Son, the only Son, and this because the Word of God assuming him became flesh, yet still assuredly remained God. Just as every man is a personal unity—that is, a unity of rational soul and flesh—so also is Christ a personal unity: Word and man.

Why should there be such great glory to a human nature—and this undoubtedly an act of grace, no merit preceding unless it be that those who consider such a question faithfully and soberly might have here a clear manifestation of God's great and sole grace, and this in order that they might understand how they themselves are justified from their sins by the selfsame grace which made it so that the man Christ had no power to sin? Thus indeed the angel hailed his mother when announcing to her the future birth: "Hail," he said, "full of grace." And shortly thereafter, "You have found favor with God."[76] And this was said of her, that she was full of grace, since she was to be mother of her Lord, indeed the Lord of all. Yet, concerning Christ himself, when the Evangelist John said, "And the Word became flesh and dwelt among us," he added, "and we beheld his glory, a glory as of the only Son of the Father, full of grace and truth."[77] When he said, "The Word was made flesh," this means, "Full of grace." When he also said, "The glory of the only begotten of the Father," this means, "Full of truth." Indeed it was Truth himself, God's only begotten Son—and, again, this not by grace but by nature—who, by grace, assumed human nature into such a personal unity that he himself became the Son of Man as well.

37. This same Jesus Christ, God's one and only Son our Lord, was born of the Holy Spirit and the Virgin Mary. Now obviously the Holy Spirit is God's gift, a gift that is itself equal to the Giver; wherefore the Holy Spirit is

God also, not inferior to the Father and the Son. Now what does this mean, that Christ's birth in respect to his human nature was of the Holy Spirit, save that this was itself also a work of grace?

For when the Virgin asked of the angel the manner by which what he announced would come to pass (since she had known no man), the angel answered: "The Holy Spirit shall come upon you and the power of the Most High shall overshadow you; therefore the Holy One which shall be born of you shall be called the Son of God."[78] And when Joseph wished to put her away, suspecting adultery (since he knew she was not pregnant by him), he received a similar answer from the angel: "Do not fear to take Mary as your wife; for that which is conceived in her is of the Holy Spirit"[79]—that is, "What you suspect is from another man is of the Holy Spirit."

# CHAPTER XII.

## The Role of the Holy Spirit

38. Are we, then, to say that the Holy Spirit is the Father of Christ's human nature, so that as God the Father generated the Word, so the Holy Spirit generated the human nature, and that from both natures Christ came to be one, Son of God the Father as the Word, Son of the Holy Spirit as man? Do we suppose that the Holy Spirit is his Father through begetting him of the Virgin Mary? Who would dare to say such a thing? There is no need to show by argument how many absurd consequences such a notion has, when it is so absurd in itself that no believer's ear can bear to hear it. Actually, then, as we confess our Lord Jesus Christ, who is God from God yet born as man of the Holy Spirit and the Virgin Mary, there is in each nature (in both the divine and the human) the only Son of God the Father Almighty, from whom proceeds the Holy Spirit.

How, then, do we say that Christ is born of the Holy Spirit, if the Holy Spirit did not beget him? Is it because he made him? This might be, since through our Lord Jesus Christ—in the form of God—all things were made. Yet in so far as he is man, he himself was made, even as the apostle says: "He was made of the seed of David according to the flesh."[80] But since that creature which the Virgin conceived and bore, though it was related to the Person of the Son alone, was made by the whole Trinity—for the works of the Trinity are not separable—why is the Holy Spirit named as the One who made it? Is it, perhaps, that when any One of the Three is named in connection with some divine action, the whole Trinity is to be understood as involved in that action? This is true and can be shown by examples, but we should not dwell too long on this kind of solution.

For what still concerns us is how it can be said, "Born of the Holy Spirit," when he is in no wise the Son of the Holy Spirit? Now, just because God made [*fecit*] this world, one could not say that the world is the son of God, or that it is "born" of God. Rather, one says it was "made" or "created" or "founded" or "established" by him, or however else one might like to speak of it. So, then, when we confess, "Born of the Holy Spirit and the Virgin Mary," the sense in which he is not the Son of the Holy Spirit and yet is the son of the Virgin Mary, when he was born both of him and of her, is difficult to explain. But there is no doubt as to the fact that he was not born from him as Father as he was born of her as mother.

39. Consequently we should not grant that whatever is born of something should therefore be called the son of that thing. Let us pass over the fact that a son is "born" of a man in a different sense than a hair is, or a louse, or a maw worm—none of these is a son. Let us pass over these things, since they are an unfitting analogy in so great a matter. Yet it is certain that those who are born of water and of the Holy Spirit would not properly be called sons of the water by anyone. But it does make sense to call them sons of God the Father and of Mother Church. Thus, therefore, the one born of the Holy Spirit is the son of God the Father, not of the Holy Spirit.

What we said about the hair and the other things has this much relevance, that it reminds us that not everything which is "born" of something is said to be "son" to him from which it is "born." Likewise, it does not follow that those who are called sons of someone are always said to have been born of him, since there are some who are adopted. Even those who are called "sons of Gehenna" are not born *of* it, but have been destined *for* it, just as the sons of the Kingdom are destined for that.

40. Wherefore, since a thing may be "born" of something else, yet not in the fashion of a "son," and conversely, since not everyone who is called son is born of him whose son he is called—this is the very mode in

which Christ was "born" of the Holy Spirit (yet not as a son), and of the Virgin Mary as a son—this suggests to us the grace of God by which a certain human person, no merit whatever preceding, at the very outset of his existence, was joined to the Word of God in such a unity of person that the selfsame one who is Son of Man should be Son of God, and the one who is Son of God should be Son of Man. Thus, in his assumption of human nature, grace came to be natural to that nature, allowing no power to sin. This is why grace is signified by the Holy Spirit, because he himself is so perfectly God that he is also called God's Gift. Still, to speak adequately of this—even if one could—would call for a very long discussion.

# CHAPTER XIII.

## Baptism and Original Sin

41. Since he was begotten and conceived in no plea-sure of carnal appetite—and therefore bore no trace of original sin—he was, by the grace of God (operating in a marvelous and an ineffable manner), joined and united in a personal unity with the only-begotten Word of the Father, a Son not by grace but by nature. And although he himself committed no sin, yet because of "the like-ness of sinful flesh"[81] in which he came, he was himself called sin and was made a sacrifice for the washing away of sins.

Indeed, under the old law, sacrifices for sins were often called sins.[82] Yet he of whom those sacrifices were mere shadows was himself actually made sin. Thus, when the apostle said, "For Christ's sake, we beseech you to be reconciled to God," he straightway added, "Him, who knew no sin, he made to be sin for us that we might be made to be the righteousness of God in him."[83] He does not say, as we read in some defective copies, "He who knew no sin did sin for us," as if Christ himself commit-ted sin for our sake. Rather, he says, "He [Christ] who knew no sin, he [God] made to be sin for us." The God to whom we are to be reconciled hath thus made him the sacrifice for sin by which we may be reconciled.

He himself is therefore sin as we ourselves are righteousness—not our own but God's, not in ourselves but in him. Just as he was sin—not his own but ours, rooted not in himself but in us—so he showed forth through the likeness of sinful flesh, in which he was crucified, that since sin was not in him he could then, so to say, die to sin by dying in the flesh, which was "the likeness of sin." And since he had never lived in the old manner of sinning, he might, in his resurrection, signify the new life which is ours, which is springing to life anew from the old death in which we had been dead to sin.

42. This is the meaning of the great sacrament of baptism, which is celebrated among us. All who attain to this grace die thereby to sin—as he himself is said to have died to sin because he died in the flesh, that is, "in the likeness of sin"—and they are thereby alive by being reborn in the baptismal font, just as he rose again from the sepulcher. This is the case no matter what the age of the body.

43. For whether it be a newborn infant or a decrepit old man—since no one should be barred from baptism—just so, there is no one who does not die to sin in baptism. Infants die to original sin only; adults, to all those sins

which they have added, through their evil living, to the burden they brought with them at birth.

44. But even these are frequently said to die to sin, when without doubt they die not to one but to many sins, and to all the sins which they have themselves already committed by thought, word, and deed. Actually, by the use of the singular number the plural number is often signified, as the poet said,

*"And they fill the belly with the armed warrior,"*[84]

although they did this with many warriors. And in our own Scriptures we read: "Pray therefore to the Lord that he may take from us the serpent."[85] It does not say "serpents," as it might, for they were suffering from many serpents. There are, moreover, innumerable other such examples.

Yet, when the original sin is signified by the use of the plural number, as we say when infants are baptized "unto the remission of sins," instead of saying "unto the remission of sin," then we have the converse expression in which the singular is expressed by the plural number. Thus in the Gospel, it is said of Herod's death, "For they are dead who sought the child's life"[86]; it does not say, "He is dead." And in Exodus: "They made," [Moses] says, "to themselves gods of gold," when they had made one calf. And of this calf, they said: "These are thy gods, O Israel, which brought you out of the land of Egypt,"[87] here also putting the plural for the singular.

45. Still, even in that one sin—which "entered into the world by one man and so spread to all men,"[88] and on account of which infants are baptized—one can recognize a plurality of sins, if that single sin is divided, so to say, into its separate elements. For there is pride in it, since man preferred to be under his own rule rather than the rule of God; and sacrilege too, for man did not acknowledge God; and murder, since he cast himself down to death; and spiritual fornication, for the integrity of the human mind was corrupted by the seduction of the serpent; and theft, since the forbidden fruit was snatched; and avarice, since he hungered for more than should have sufficed for him—and whatever other sins that could be discovered in the diligent analysis of that one sin.

46. It is also said—and not without support—that infants are involved in the sins of their parents, not only of the first pair, but even of their own, of whom they were born. Indeed, that divine judgment, "I shall visit the sins of the fathers on their children,"[89] definitely applies to them before they come into the New Covenant by regeneration. This Covenant was foretold by Ezekiel

when he said that the sons should not bear their fathers' sins, nor the proverb any longer apply in Israel, "Our fathers have eaten sour grapes and the children's teeth are set on edge."[90]

This is why each one of them must be born again, so that he may thereby be absolved of whatever sin was in him at the time of birth. For the sins committed by evil-doing after birth can be healed by repentance—as, indeed, we see it happen even after baptism. For the new birth [*regeneratio*] would not have been instituted except for the fact that the first birth [*generatio*] was tainted—and to such a degree that one born of even a lawful wedlock said, "I was conceived in iniquities; and in sins did my mother nourish me in her womb."[91] Nor did he say "in iniquity" or "in sin," as he might have quite correctly; rather, he preferred to say "iniquities" and "sins," because, as I explained above, there are so many sins in that one sin—which has passed into all men, and which was so great that human nature was changed and by it brought under the necessity of death—and also because there are other sins, such as those of parents, which, even if they cannot change our nature in the same way, still involve the children in guilt, unless the gracious grace and mercy of God interpose.

47. But, in the matter of the sins of one's other parents, those who stand as one's forebears from Adam down

to one's own parents, a question might well be raised: whether a man at birth is involved in the evil deeds of all his forebears, and their multiplied original sins, so that the later in time he is born, the worse estate he is born in; or whether, on this very account, God threatens to visit the sins of the parents as far as—but no farther than—the third and fourth generations, because in his mercy he will not continue his wrath beyond that. It is not his purpose that those not given the grace of regeneration be crushed under too heavy a burden in their eternal damnation, as they would be if they were bound to bear, as original guilt, all the sins of their ancestors from the beginning of the human race, and to pay the due penalty for them. Whether yet another solution to so difficult a problem might or might not be found by a more diligent search and interpretation of Holy Scripture, I dare not rashly affirm.

# CHAPTER XIV.

# The Mysteries of Christ's Mediatorial Work and Justification

48. That one sin, however, committed in a setting of such great happiness, was itself so great that by it, in one man, the whole human race was originally and, so to say, radically condemned. It cannot be pardoned and washed away except through "the one mediator between God and men, the man Christ Jesus,"[92] who alone could be born in such a way as not to need to be reborn.

49. They were not reborn, those who were baptized by John's baptism, by which Christ himself was baptized.[93] Rather, they were *prepared* by the ministry of this forerunner, who said, "Prepare a way for the Lord,"[94] for Him in whom alone they could be reborn.

For his baptism is not with water alone, as John's was, but with the Holy Spirit as well. Thus, whoever believes in Christ is reborn by that same Spirit, of whom Christ also was born, needing not to be reborn. This is the reason for the Voice of the Father spoken over him at his baptism, "Today have I begotten thee,"[95] which pointed not to that particular day on which he was baptized, but to that "day" of changeless eternity, in order to show us that this Man belonged to the personal Unity of the Only Begotten. For a day that neither begins with the close of yesterday nor ends with the beginning of tomorrow is indeed an eternal "today."

Therefore, he chose to be baptized in water by John, not thereby to wash away any sin of his own, but to manifest his great humility. Indeed, baptism found nothing in him to wash away, just as death found nothing to punish. Hence, it was in authentic justice, and not by violent power, that the devil was overcome and conquered: for, as he had most unjustly slain Him who was in no way deserving of death, he also did most justly lose those whom he had justly held in bondage as punishment for their sins. Wherefore, He took upon himself both baptism and death, not out of a piteous necessity but through his own free act of showing mercy—as part of a definite plan whereby One might take away the sin of the world, just as one man had brought sin into the world, that is, the whole human race.

50. There is a difference, however. The first man brought sin into the world, whereas this One took away not only that one sin but also all the others which he found added to it. Hence, the apostle says, "And the gift [of grace] is not like the effect of the one that

sinned: for the judgment on that one trespass was condemnation; but the gift of grace is for many offenses,
and brings justification."[96] Now it is clear that the one
sin originally inherited, even if it were the only one
involved, makes men liable to condemnation. Yet grace
justifies a man for many offenses, both the sin which he
originally inherited in common with all the others and
also the multitude of sins which he has committed on
his own.

51. However, when he [the apostle] says, shortly after,
"Therefore, as the offense of one man led all men to
condemnation, so also the righteousness of one man
leads all men to the life of justification,"[97] he indicates
sufficiently that everyone born of Adam is subject to
damnation, and no one, unless reborn of Christ, is free
from such a damnation.

52. And after this discussion of punishment through
one man and grace through the Other, as he deemed
sufficient for that part of the epistle, the apostle passes
on to speak of the great mystery of holy baptism in the
cross of Christ, and to do this so that we may understand
nothing other in the baptism of Christ than the likeness
of the death of Christ. The death of Christ crucified
is nothing other than the likeness of the forgiveness of
sins—so that in the very same sense in which the death
is real, so also is the forgiveness of our sins real, and in

the same sense in which his resurrection is real, so also in us is there authentic justification.

He asks: "What, then, shall we say? Shall we continue in sin, that grace may abound?"[98]—for he had previously said, "But where sin abounded, grace did much more abound."[99] And therefore he himself raised the question whether, because of the abundance of grace that follows sin, one should then continue in sin. But he answers, "God forbid!" and adds, "How shall we, who are dead to sin, live any longer therein?"[100] Then, to show that we are dead to sin, "Do you not know that all we who were baptized in Christ Jesus were baptized into his death?"[101]

If, therefore, the fact that we are baptized into the death of Christ shows that we are dead to sin, then certainly infants who are baptized in Christ die to sin, since they are baptized into his own death. For there is no exception in the saying, "All we who are baptized into Christ Jesus are baptized into his death." And the effect of this is to show that we are dead to sin.

Yet what sin do infants die to in being reborn except that which they inherit in being born? What follows in the epistle also pertains to this: "Therefore we were buried with him by baptism into death; that, as Christ was raised up from the dead by the glory of the Father, even so we also should walk in the newness of life. For if we have been united with him in the likeness of his death, we shall be also united with him in the likeness of his resurrection, knowing this, that our old man is crucified with him, that the body of sin might be destroyed, that henceforth we should not serve sin. For he that is dead is freed from sin. Now if we are dead with Christ, we believe that we shall also live with him: knowing that Christ, being raised from the dead, dies no more; death has no more dominion over him. For the death he died, he died to sin, once for all; but the life he lives, he lives unto God. So also, reckon yourselves also to be dead to sin, but alive unto God through Christ Jesus."[102]

Now, he had set out to prove that we should not go on sinning, in order that thereby grace might abound, and had said, "If we have died to sin, how, then, shall we go on living in it?" And then to show that we were dead to sin, he had added, "Know you not, that as many of us as were baptized into Jesus Christ were baptized into his death?" Thus he concludes the passage as he began it. Indeed, he introduced the death of Christ in order to say that even he died to sin. To what sin, save that of the flesh in which he existed, not as sinner, but in "the likeness of sin" and which was, therefore, called by the name of sin? Thus, to those baptized into the death of Christ—into which not only adults but infants as well are baptized—he says, "So also you should reckon yourselves to be dead to sin, but alive to God in Christ Jesus."

53. Whatever was done, therefore, in the crucifixion of Christ, his burial, his resurrection on the third day, his ascension into heaven, his being seated at the Father's right hand—all these things were done thus, that they might not only signify their mystical meanings but also serve as a model for the Christian life which we lead here on the earth. Thus, of his crucifixion it was said, "And they that are Jesus Christ's have crucified their own flesh, with the passions and lusts thereof"[103]; and of his burial, "For we are buried with Christ by baptism into death"; of his resurrection, "Since Christ is raised from the dead through the glory of the Father, so we also should walk with him in newness of life"; of his ascension and session at the Father's right hand: "But if you have risen again with Christ, seek the things which are above, where Christ is sitting at the right hand of God. Set your affection on things above, not on things on the earth. For you are dead, and your life is hid with Christ in God."[104]

54. Now what we believe concerning Christ's future actions, since we confess that he will come again from heaven to judge the living and the dead, does not pertain to this life of ours as we live it here on earth, because it belongs not to his deeds already done, but to what

he will do at the close of the age. To this the apostle refers and goes on to add, "When Christ, who is your life, shall appear, you shall then also appear with him in glory."[105]

55. There are two ways to interpret the affirmation that he "shall judge the living and the dead." On the one hand, we may understand by "the living" those who are not yet dead but who will be found living in the flesh when he comes; and we may understand by "the dead" those who have left the body, or who shall have left it before his coming. Or, on the other hand, "the living" may signify "the righteous," and "the dead" may signify "the unrighteous"—since the righteous are to be judged as well as the unrighteous. For sometimes the judgment of God is passed upon the evil, as in the word, "But they who have done evil [shall come forth] to the resurrection of judgment."[106] And sometimes it is passed upon the good, as in the word, "Save me, O God, by thy name, and judge me in thy strength."[107] Indeed, it is by the judgment of God that the distinction between good and evil is made, to the end that, being freed from evil and not destroyed with the evildoers, the good may be set apart at his right hand.[108] This is why the psalmist cried, "Judge me, O God," and, as if to explain what he had said, "and defend my cause against an unholy nation."[109]

# NOTES

## CHAPTER I.

1. 1 Cor. 1:20.
2. Wis. 6:26 (Vulgate).
3. Rom. 16:19.
4. A later interpolation, not found in the best MSS., adds, "As no one can exist from himself, so also no one can be wise in himself save only as he is enlightened by Him of whom it is written, 'All wisdom is from God' [Ecclus. 1:1]."
5. Job 28:28.
6. A transliteration of the Greek ἐγχειρίδιον, literally, a handbook or manual.
7. Cf. Gal. 5:6.
8. Cf. 1 Cor. 13:10, 11.
9. 1 Cor. 3:11.
10. Already, very early in his ministry (397), Augustine had written *De agone Christiano*, in which he had reviewed and refuted a full score of heresies threatening the orthodox faith.

## CHAPTER II.

11. The Apostles' Creed. Cf. Augustine's early essay *On Faith and the Creed*.
12. Joel 2:32.
13. Rom. 10:14.
14. Lucan, *Pharsalia*, II, 15.
15. Virgil, *Aeneid*, IV, 419. The context of this quotation is Dido's lament over Aeneas' prospective abandonment of her. She is saying that if she could have foreseen such a disaster, she would have been able to bear it. Augustine's criticism here is a literalistic quibble.

16. Heb. 11:1.

17. *Sacra eloquia*—a favorite phrase of Augustine's for the Bible.

18. Rom. 8:24, 25 (Old Latin).

19. James 2:19.

## CHAPTER III.

20. One of the standard titles of early Greek philosophical treatises was [[pi]] [[epsilon]] [[rho]] [[iota]] [[phi]][[nu]][[sigma]][[epsilon]][[omega]][[zeta]], which would translate into Latin as *De rerum natura*. This is, in fact, the title of Lucretius' famous poem, the greatest philosophical work written in classical Latin.

21. This basic motif appears everywhere in Augustine's thought as the very foundation of his whole system.

22. This section (Chs. III and IV) is the most explicit statement of a major motif which pervades the whole of Augustinian metaphysics. We see it in his earliest writings, *Soliloquies*, 1, 2, and *De ordine*, II, 7. It is obviously a part of the Neoplatonic heritage which Augustine appropriated for his Christian philosophy. The good is positive, constructive, essential; evil is privative, destructive, parasitic on the good. It has its origin, not in nature, but in the will. Cf. *Confessions*, Bk. VII, Chs. III, V, XII–XVI; *On Continence*, 14–16; *On the Gospel of John*, Tractate XCVIII, 7; *City of God*, XI, 17; XII, 7–9.

## CHAPTER IV.

23. Isa. 5:20.

24. Matt. 12:35.

25. This refers to Aristotle's well-known principle of "the excluded middle."

26. Matt. 7:18.

27. Cf. Matt. 12:33.

## CHAPTER V.

28. Virgil, *Georgios*, II, 490.

29. *Ibid.*, 479.

30. *Sed in via pedum, non in via morum.*

31. Virgil, *Eclogue*, VIII, 42. The context of the passage is Damon's complaint over his faithless Nyssa; he is here remembering the first time he ever saw her—when he was twelve! Cf. *Theocritus*, II, 82.

32. Cf. Matt. 5:37.

33. Cf. Confessions, Bk. X, Ch. XXIII.

## CHAPTER VI.

34. *Ad consentium contra mendacium*, CSEL (J. Zycha, ed.), Vol. 41, pp. 469–528; also Migne, PL, 40, c. 517–548; English translation by H.B. Jaffee in Deferrari, *St. Augustine: Treatises on Various Subjects* (The Fathers of the Church, New York, 1952), pp. 113–179. This had been written about a year earlier than the *Enchiridion*. Augustine had also written another treatise *On Lying* much earlier, c. 395; see *De mendacio in CSEL* (J. Zycha, ed.), Vol. 41, pp. 413–466; Migne, PL, 40, c. 487-518; English translation by M.S. Muldowney in Deferrari, *op. cit.*, pp. 47-109. This summary of his position here represents no change of view whatever on this question.

35. Sallust, *The War with Catiline*, X, 6–7.

## CHAPTER VII.

36. Cf. Acts 12:9.

37. Virgil, *Aeneid*, X, 392.

38. This refers to one of the first of the Cassiciacum dialogues, *Contra Academicos*. The gist of Augustine's refutation of skepticism is in III, 23ff. Throughout his whole career he continued to maintain this position: that certain knowledge begins with self-knowledge. Cf. *Confessions*, Bk.V, Ch. X, 19; see also *City of God*, XI, xxvii.

39. Hab. 2:4; Rom. 1:17.
40. A direct contrast between *suspensus assenso*—the watch word of the Academics—and *assensio*, the badge of Christian certitude.
41. See above, VII, 90.
42. Matt. 5:37.
43. Matt. 6:12.

## CHAPTER VIII.

44. Rom. 5:12.

## CHAPTER IX.

45. Cf. Luke 20:36.
46. Rom. 4:17.
47. Wis. 11:20.
48. 2 Peter 2:19.
49. John 8:36
50. Eph. 2:8.
51. 1 Cor. 7:25.
52. Eph. 2:8, 9.
53. Eph. 2:10.
54. Cf. Gal. 6:15; 2 Cor. 5:17.
55. Ps. 51:10.
56. Phil. 2:13.
57. Rom. 9:16.
58. Prov. 8:35 (LXX).
59. From the days at Cassiciacum till the very end, Augustine toiled with the mystery of the primacy of God's grace and the reality of human freedom. Of two things he was unwaveringly sure, even though they involved him in a paradox and the appearance of confusion. The first is that God's grace is not only primary but also sufficient as the ground and source of human willing. And against the Pelagians and other detractors from grace, he did not hesitate to insist that grace is irresistible and inviolable. Cf. *On Grace and Free Will*, 99, 41–43; *On the Predestination of*

*the Saints*, 19:10; *On the Gift of Perseverance*, 41; *On the Soul and Its Origin*, 16; and even the *Enchiridion*, XXIV, 97.

But he never drew from this deterministic emphasis the conclusion that man is unfree and everywhere roundly rejects the not illogical corollary of his theonomism, that man's will counts for little or nothing except as passive agent of God's will. He insists on responsibility on man's part in responding to the initiatives of grace. For this emphasis, which is characteristically directed to the faithful themselves, see *On the Psalms*, LXVIII, 7–8; *On the Gospel of John*, Tractate, 53:6–8; and even his severest anti-Pelagian tracts: *On Grace and Free Will*, 6–8, 10, 31 and *On Admonition and Grace*, 2–8.

60. Ps. 58:11 (Vulgate).

61. Ps. 23:6.

62. Cf. Matt. 5:44.

63. The theme that he had explored in *Confessions*, Bks. I–IX. See especially Bk. V, Chs. X, XIII; Bk. VII, Ch. VIII; Bk. IX, Ch. I.

### CHAPTER X.

64. Cf. Ps. 90:9.

65. Job 14:1.

66. John 3:36.

67. Eph. 2:3.

68. Rom. 5:9, 10.

69. Rom. 8:14.

70. John 1:14.

71. Rom. 3:20.

72. *Epistle* CXXXVII, written in 412 in reply to a list of queries sent to Augustine by the proconsul of Africa.

73. John 1:1.

74. Phil. 2:6, 7.

75. These metaphors for contrasting the "two natures" of Jesus Christ were favorite figures of speech in Augustine's Christological thought. Cf. *On the Gospel of John*, Tractate

78; *On the Trinity*, I, 7; II, 2; IV, 19–20; VII, 3; *New Testament Sermons*, 76, 14.

## CHAPTER XI.
76. Luke 1:28–30.
77. John 1:14.
78. Luke 1:35.
79. Matt. 1:20.

## CHAPTER XII.
80. Rom. 1:3.

## CHAPTER XIII.
81. Rom. 8:3.
82. Cf. Hos. 4:8.
83. 2 Cor. 5:20, 21.
84. Virgil, *Aeneid*, II, 1, 20.
85. Num. 21:7 (LXX).
86. Matt. 2:20.
87. Ex. 32:4.
88. Rom. 5:12.
89. Deut. 5:9.
90. Ezek. 18:2.
91. Ps. 51:5.

## CHAPTER XIV.
92. 1 Tim. 2:5.
93. Matt. 3:13.
94. Luke 3:4; Isa. 40:3.
95. Ps. 2:7; Heb. 5:5; cf. Mark 1:9–11.
96. Rom. 5:16.
97. Rom. 5:18.
98. Rom. 6:1.
99. Rom. 5:20.
100.Rom. 6:2.
101. Rom. 6:3.

102. Rom. 6:4–11.
103. Gal. 5:24.
104. Col. 3:1–3.
105. Col. 3:4.
106. John 5:29.
107. Ps. 54:1.
108. Cf. Matt. 25:32, 33.
109. Ps. 43:1.